Love is Patient
Love is Kind
Coloring Book

Jessica Mazurkiewicz

DOVER PUBLICATIONS
Garden City, New York

Enhance the beauty of scripture with color! Inside this book you'll find more than 60 illustrations to inspire you, each containing a faith-strengthening Bible verse from the book of Psalms, Proverbs, and more. Each scripture is beautifully adorned with flowers, songbirds, or inspiring scenes reminiscent of paradise just waiting to be filled with color. As you use your artistic touch, the words will come alive, offering you comfort, peace, and hours of enjoyment.

This Dover edition, first published in 2023, is a new selection of artwork from the following coloring books by Jessica Mazurkiewicz: *Creative Haven Inspiring Proverbs* (2018), *Creative Haven Psalms* (2018), and *Creative Haven Beautiful Bible Blessings* (2020).

ISBN-13: 978-0-486-85336-9
ISBN-10: 0-486-85336-5

Manufactured in the United States of America
85336501   2023
www.doverpublications.com

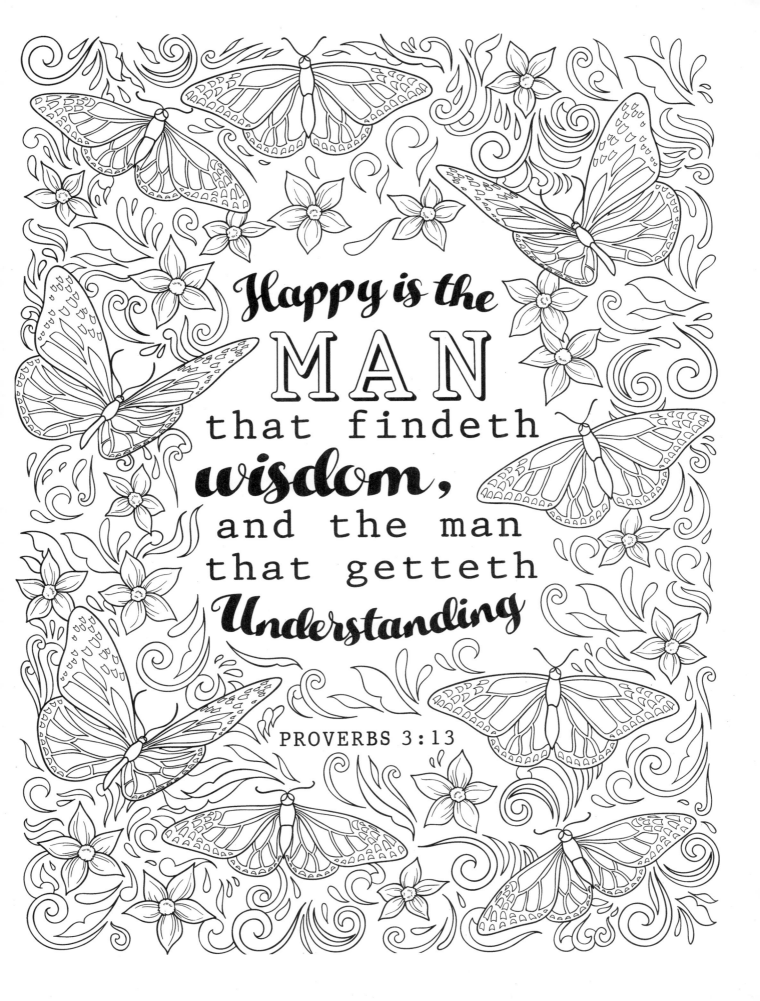

Happy is the
MAN
that findeth
wisdom,
and the man
that getteth
Understanding

PROVERBS 3:13

COME NEAR
to God,
and he will come
NEAR TO YOU

JAMES 4:8

But the meek shall inherit the earth and delight themselves in the abundance of peace

PSALM 37:11

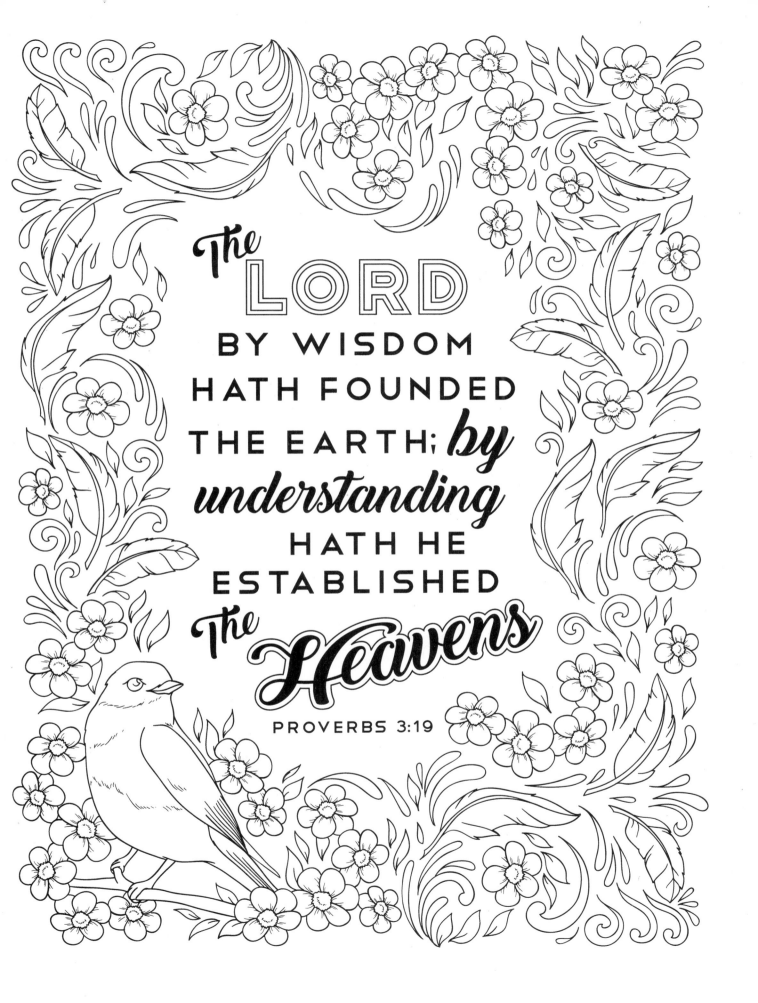

The LORD BY WISDOM HATH FOUNDED THE EARTH; by understanding HATH HE ESTABLISHED The Heavens

PROVERBS 3:19

I will praise thee for I am fearfully and wonderfully made

Marvellous are thy works and that my soul knoweth right well

PSALM 139:14

FOR WE WALK

by faith

NOT

by sight

2 CORINTHIANS 5:7

The voice of the LORD is upon the waters

PSALM 29:3

Train up
a child
in the way
he should go:
and when
he is old,
he will not
depart from it

PROVERBS 22:6

The LORD will give strength unto his people the LORD will bless his people with peace

PSALM 29:11

KEEP MY COMMANDMENTS, and live; AND MY LAW AS the apple of thine eye

PROVERBS 7:2

ABOVE ALL

love

EACH OTHER DEEPLY, BECAUSE

love

COVERS A MULTITUDE OF SINS

1 PETER 4:8

Say unto WISDOM, THOU ART MY SISTER; and call UNDERSTANDING THY KINSWOMAN

Proverbs 7:4

Don't be Afraid, Just Believe

MARK 5:36

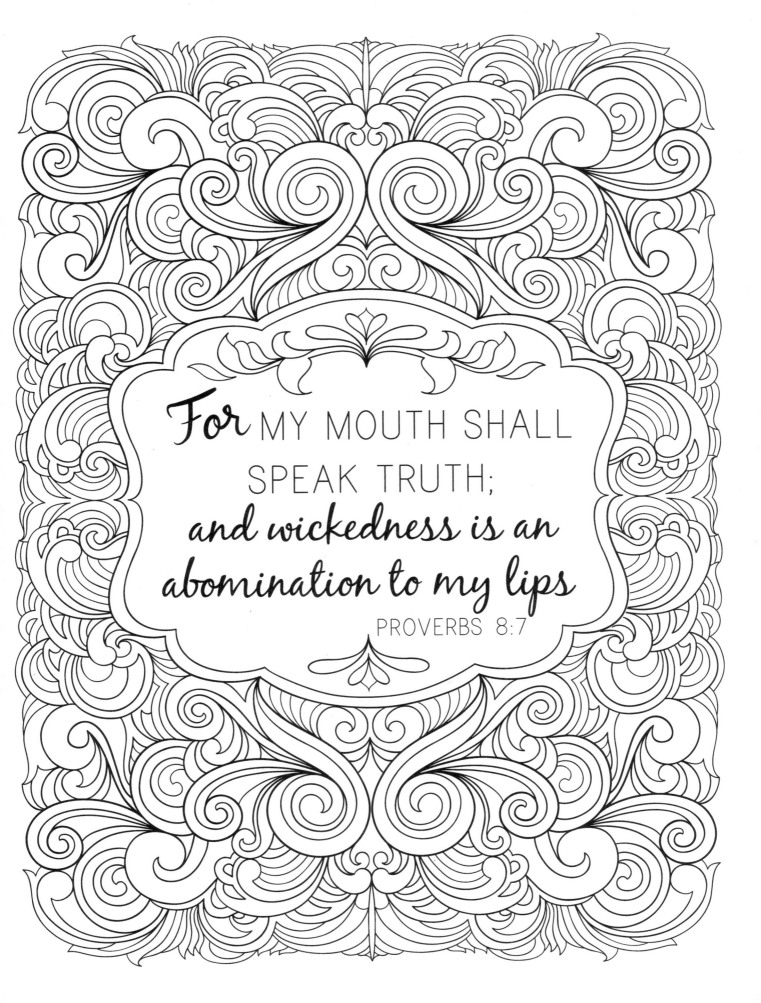

For MY MOUTH SHALL SPEAK TRUTH; and wickedness is an abomination to my lips

PROVERBS 8:7

I am with you
and will watch
over you
wherever you go

GENESIS 28:15

The heavens declare the glory of God and the firmament sheweth his handywork

PSALM 19:1

A wise man
is strong; yea,
a man of
knowledge
increaseth
strength

Proverbs 24:5

The LORD hath done great things for us

Thereof we are glad

PSALM 126:3

I love them that love me; and those that seek me early shall find me

Proverbs 8:17

Before the mountains
were settled,
before the hills
was I brought forth

PROVERBS 8:25

Love is patient, love is kind

1 CORINTHIANS 13:4

He healeth the broken in heart and bindeth up their wounds

PSALM 147:3

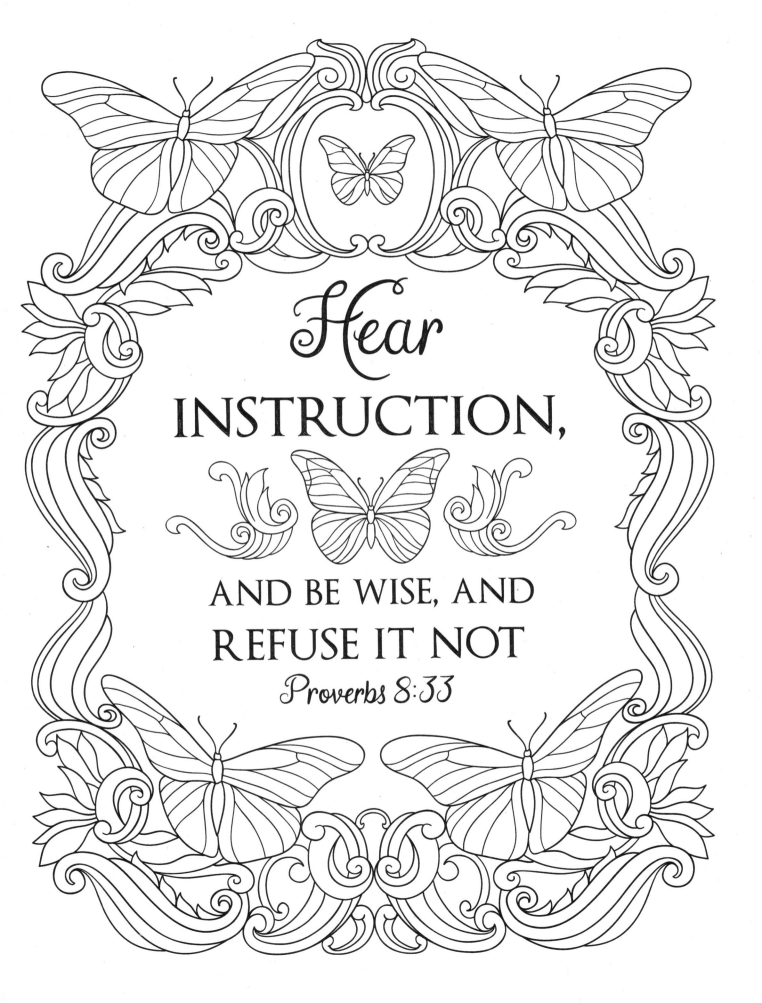

Hear
INSTRUCTION,
AND BE WISE, AND
REFUSE IT NOT
Proverbs 8:33

For whoso
findeth me
findeth life, and
shall obtain favour
of the Lord

PROVERBS 8:35

For this God is our
God forever and ever

He will be our guide
even unto death

PSALM 48:14

HATRED *stirreth up* **strifes:** **BUT LOVE** COVERETH *all sins*

PROVERBS 10:12

A Gracious wOMAN RETAINETH HONOUR: and strong men retain RICHES

Proverbs 11:16

Our help is in the name of the LORD who made heaven and earth

PSALM 124:8

A soft answer turneth away wrath: but grievous words stir up anger

PROVERBS 15:1

A merry heart maketh a cheerful countenance: but by sorrow of the heart the spirit is broken

Proverbs 15:13

FOR HIS ANGER ENDURETH BUT A MOMENT; IN HIS FAVOUR IS LIFE: WEEPING MAY ENDURE FOR A NIGHT BUT JOY COMETH IN THE MORNING

PSALM 30:5

All the ways of a man are clean in his own eyes; but the LORD weigheth the spirits

Proverbs 16:2

I CAN DO ALL THIS THROUGH HIM WHO GIVES ME STRENGTH

PHILIPPIANS 4:13

A man's **heart**
deviseth his way:
but the **LORD**
directeth his *steps*
Proverbs 16:9

He has
made
EVERYTHING
beautiful
in its time

ECCLESIASTES 3:11

A friend loveth at all times, and a brother is born for adversity

PROVERBS 17:17

LOOK TO THE LORD AND HIS STRENGTH SEEK HIS FACE ALWAYS

1 CHRONICLES 16:11

This is the day
which the LORD
hath made

We will rejoice
and be glad in it

PSALM 118:24

THE JUST MAN WALKETH IN HIS INTEGRITY His CHILDREN ARE BLESSED AFTER HIM

PROVERBS 20:7